INSPIRATIONS FROM SWAMI VIVEKANANDA

Young India Library

Inspirations From Swami Vivekananda

Parables for Young Readers

SHEKHAR SARKAR

Foreword by
PROF P YASH PAL
Former Chairman, University Grants Commission

Illustrations
NEETA GANGOPADHYAY

nbt.india
एकः सूते सकलम्

NATIONAL BOOK TRUST, INDIA

First Edition Published in 2015
Reprints 2015, 2017, 2019, 2020, 2021, 2022, 2025 (Saka 1947)
by the Director, National Book Trust, India
5 Institutional Area, Vasant Kunj, New Delhi-110070
Website: www.nbtindia.gov.in

Agartala • Bengaluru • Bhopal • Chennai
Cuttack • Dehradun • Guwahati • Hyderabad
Kochi • Kolkata • Lucknow • Mumbai • Patna

ISBN 978-81-237-7381-0

₹ 100.00

Printed at Chandu Press, Delhi

Seek and thee shall find ...
Work and thee shall succeed!

Contents

A few simple words have deeper meaning than complex meaningless words.

Foreword

I am delighted and intrigued by the way in which the brilliant inspirational words of Swami Vivekananda have been presented by Shekhar Sarkar, in this National Book Trust, Young India Library series publication – *Inspirations from Swami Vivekananda: Parables for Young Readers.*

Good wishes for more words of such inspirations for the new generation young readers.

Professor Yash Pal
Former Chairman, UGC

15-1-2015

Padma Vibhushan Prof P. Yash Pal is an internationally acclaimed Indian scientist and educator. He is known for his contributions to the study of cosmic rays, as well as for being an institution-builder. He is the former Chairman of University Grants Commission.

Swami Vivekananda learnt from his master Sri Ramkrishna Paramahansa the method to evolve a new paradigm of knowledge to transcend beyond the periphery of esoteric human knowledge to seek the 'Absolute Perfection and Unity' in the duality of every entity.

He found in the Advaitic knowledge the need for the amelioration of the humans towards perfection; not in spirituality, but in social wealth investments, that could nurture the humane approach to rational positive outlook in society, and ignite the scientific temper, so as to expand the space for 'Human Values' progressively, to seek that 'Perfection'.

Inspirational Thinkers on Swami Vivekananda

I have gone through Vivekananda's works very thoroughly, and after having gone through them, the love I had for my country became thousand fold.

- Mahatma Gandhi

Rooted in the past, full of pride in India's prestige, Vivekananda was yet modern in his approach to life's problems, and was a kind of bridge between the past of India and her present ... he came as a tonic to the depressed and demoralized Hindu mind and gave it self-reliance and some roots in the past.

- **Pandit Jawahar Lal Nehru**

Vivekananda not only made us conscious of our strength, he also pointed out our defects and drawbacks. He taught us : 'The same soul resides in each and all. If you are convinced of this,it is your duty to treat all as brothers and serve mankind'

- Vinoba Bhave

Swamiji harmonized the East and the West, religion and science, past and present. And that is why he is great. Our countrymen have gained unprecedented self-respect, self-reliance and self-assertion from his teachings.

- Netaji Subhash Chandra Bose

If you want to know India, study Vivekananda. In him everything is positive, nothing negative

- Rabindranath Tagore

We perceive Vivekanada's influence still working gigantically, we know not well how, we known not well where, in something that is not yet formed,something leonine, something grand,intuitive, upheaving that has entered the soul of India and we say 'Be hold,Vivekanada still lives in the soul of his Mother and in the soul of her children'

- Sri Aurobindo

He told us : Do not be led away from appearances. Deep down there is a providential will, there is a purpose in this universe.You must try to co-operate with that purpose and try to achieve it.

- **Dr S Radahakrishnan**

Author's Note

I was always intrigued by Swami Vivekananda's thoughts. However, wisdom dawned a decade ago when Swami Gokulanand of Ramkrishna Mission graced my residence in New Delhi. He was kind to candidly discuss the 'enigmatic' side of Swami Vivekananda.

In recent time, my discussion with the former UGC Chairman, Prof Yash Pal at his residence on 'scientific temper', gave me a new acuity on Swami Vivekananda's 'Advaita' principle to seek unity, by integration into every entity; a 'rational-emotional' complementary approach to refine human values.

I have since admired Swami Vivekananda as a nationalist, rationalist, empiricist and positivist, but more as a humanist who promoted the *'Advaita'* precept of unity, and the natural 'will' of humans.

Swami Vivekananda's personal observations and enquiry during his formative years, ignited the scientific temper in the natural 'will' to help young Narendra inquisitively seek, and resolve the *'rational-emotional strife'* as 'cognitive consciousness' within him, by the process of elimination of 'falsehood', and in the acceptance of 'Truth' with a free mind.

The young Narendra's skeptical query to his mystic master Swami Ramkrishna Parmahansa on 'existence' and 'maya', was not to seek spirituality, but an evolving scientific temperament to seek the truth in every entity; a human sensibility enabling the young mind in the process of knowledge acquisition in familiar environment, to grout learning on the reality of the land and his environment, without sacrificing the essence of existence and human values.

Sister Nivedita, a disciple, sums up 'the young Narendra' as: *'young, tumultuous, overflowing with its own energy and self-assurance, yet inquisitive and alert withal'*.

The relevance of Swami Vivekananda's inspirations, in this age of information dissemination and surge in technology, could help children learn to associate their *'cognitive consciousness'* with the logic of choice from the long term memory gathered through their life , and judiciously apply them as skills, by using tactile activities to foster creativity. This exciting adventure of discovery in children, ignites the latent 'scientific temper' as positive attitude, away from distractions to a focused mind, required in our contemporary times.

Jawaharlal Nehru, a visionary and advocator of 'scientific temper' also resonates Swami Vivekananda's views in his book –*The Discovery of India*:

> *'What is needed is the scientific approach, the adventurous and yet critical temper of science, the search for truth and new knowledge, the refusal to accept anything without testing and trial, the capacity to change previous conclusions in the face of new*

evidence, the reliance on observed fact and not on pre-conceived theory, the hard discipline of the mind—all this is necessary, not merely for the application of science but for life itself and the solution of its many problems.'

I feel inspired to write this book titled *Inspirations from Swami Vivekananda: Parables for Young Readers*, as a National Book Trust publication, under the Ministry of HRD, in reviving the scientific temper as a 'touch stone' for human values, as envisaged by Swami Vivekananda for our new generation young readers.

SHEKHAR SARKAR

INTRODUCTION

INTRODUCTION
For Teachers & Parents

Doing is very good, but that comes from thinking. Little manifestations of energy through the muscles are called work. But where there is no thought, there will be no work. Fill the brain, therefore with high thoughts, highest ideals, place them day and night before you, and out of that will come great work.

Stand up, be bold, and be strong. Take the whole responsibility on your own shoulders, and know that you are the creator of your own destiny. All the strength and succour you want is within yourselves. Therefore, make your own future.

- Swami Vivekananda

Since antiquity, philosophies have aimed to reveal hidden assumptions of existence and life. Civilizations have evolved and perished, but traced in later periods in historical artifacts, relics, mythologies, legends, traditions, customs, culture and religion - often in veiled allegory of existence and the resonance of inner life. Swami Vivekananda does not advocate death or after life as discourse in spirituality, but the '*providential will*' within every human striving for perfection in existence.

Vivekanandism is not a philosophy founded on antiquity, but a way of life - *to make bad humans good, and good humans better. In a way it alludes to the Darwinian principle of the 'natural will' in the struggle and evolution of life and existence. In brief, Swami Vivekanada's arduous endeavor was to build a better human, better society, and a better nation.* It was an attempt to unfold the wisdom of existence and life in every entity.

Numerous biographies on Swami Vivekananda unfold accomplishments during his personal life; apart from the sloganism and iconization of Swami Vivekananda as a Vedantic monk and youth leader. Compendium of nebulous sermons and proverbs as words of wisdom are published. However, only a miniscule focus on the real essence of lifetime *'values'* as instructions of Swami Vivekananda on being a better human, and on the method of transforming oneself as asset in society.

The *'value dimensions'* in Swami Vivekananda's teachings and his thoughts, so relevant in our contemporary times, are both apolitical and secular, with Universal ethos for our children, youth and adults. He preaches no ancient philosophy or religion.

He gleans the quintessence of existence from human history and ancient scriptures. He attempts to find unity in all aspects of life with the 'infinite' pristine perfect self.

'Value dimensions' of humans are not mere sermons of morality, neither spirituality to gain *'Moksha'*, nor normative views of existence in illusionism, but a practical approach in rationalizing the *'cognitive consciousness'*

in making decisions between choices- to garner all human *'values'*; in refining one's personality and deportment; in the right choice of a profession according to one's potential, and in the optimization of ability and skills for a career that gives satisfaction and dignity of work, with socio-economic benefits. The dignity of humans and pride of a nation was his *tumultuous* effort and ardent passion.

'Values' are holistic in nature, and viewed from different planes by each player with enhanced utility, in the process of optimization. In short, it is the individual's effort in the realization of the perfect truth about one's potential, and the world to recognize it. It raises the bar in the qualitative aspects of existence.

The modern youth unfortunately, in veiled *'falsehood'* connotes these precepts in the socio-economic hierarchy of personal 'instant' benefit, and 'instant' success. They have very little understanding of their own efforts in the important task of perfect individual development, and the task of nation building, through collaborative contribution of their endeavor. They remain self absorbed dependent individuals.

It is *faith*, *devotion*, *determination*, *sincere effort*, *perseverance*, *fearlessness*, *panache*, *brotherhood*, *righteousness*, *humility*, *mannerism and honesty*, that Swami Vivekananda through simple analogy, shows the path to overcome impediments : to rise above conceited thoughts - to live, and let live with dignity. They are the basic *'human values'* that help individuals face challenges, by rational decisions with the ability developed as life skills; to logically and conscientiously differentiate the right from the wrong. It becomes a wonderful experience for the youth to realize one's inner essence.

It is analogous to a budding flower that opens up every beautiful petal to reveal the inner fragrance- the eternal 'glow' within. This is the awakening of the 'new consciousnesses' - the eternal essence within every human being.

The *'value dimensions'* of Swami Vivekanada's inspirations are the *modern weapons for the youth to face the onslaught, the challenges of disappointments, the frustrations in their life of strife, and confusion.*

Swami Vivekanada's approach is analytical, similar to any scientific principle - to first observe and indentify the human potential, then introspect to purify the core 'values' as essence in excellence, and finally utilize the life skills as 'values' imbibed to overcome all challenges, guided by the human rationality and conscience. This unique combination of scientific temper and emotional intelligence guides the human conscience to a determined will, to negate all unproductive endeavors to proclaim- 'Yes. I can'.

'Scientific temper' is like a user friendly catalyst that participates in enquiry and change in cognitive assumptions to rational acceptance, yet remains unchanged as a rational innate human faculty. While information and technology can help design a perfect 'machine'; human values help design a perfect 'human'. The former, a mechanistic function through rigid format; the latter, a 'rational' function, with freedom of thought, guided by the conscience.

Swami Vivekananda playfully cajoles a game plan as a human focused design for the youth in good gamification, to combine serious thoughts with fun, and offer new opportunities in life as inspiration.

In brief, it is the *'talisman'* he offers to the youth for holistic development and perfection as a human being. He applies the force of one's conscience as the only principle to morality; while sincerity and hard work could sharpen the human skills to optimization of their potential, and ignite the scientific temper; the conscience would lead the path to *'Truth'*. He therefore tells the youth, to first recognize one's own human physical and mental potential, and then hone them to perfection. It is not the external environment, but the internal self to feel in shaping oneself to the realization of the truth in existence.

What I want is muscles of iron and nerves of steel, inside which dwells a mind of the same material as that of which the thunderbolt is made.

Work on with the intrepidity of a lion, but at the same time with the tenderness of a flower.

Yet, like a master 'mason' who crafts a perfect building, the speculative 'mason' as a human master craftsman, knew that *'the eye may perceive :mind conceive: heart devise, but the hands fail to execute'*. There was a need to coordinate the heart with the mind: the human emotions and passion with rationality of thought, and integrate it with the perfection of work.

To such self realization by the youth, the sage advocates them to imbibe *'values'* that enhance the quality of life - a modern perspective to freedom of thought, change in the attitude and mindset, friendship, empathy, knowledge, tenacity, compassion and perseverance; not through revolution, but evolution as change with the changing natural and social environment, in one's attitude and perspective towards life. It was to be achieved not by compromise, but by *'smoothening out the excrescencies both in traditions and modernity'*, as equitable blend.

'We must have friendship for all; we must be merciful toward those that are in misery; when people are happy, we ought to be happy; and to the wicked we must be indifferent. These attitudes will make the mind peaceful.'

'We must plunge heart and soul and body into the work. And until we are ready to sacrifice everything else to one Idea, and to one alone, we never, never will see the Light.'

'We reap what we sow. We are the makers of our own fate. None else has the blame, none has the praise....'

'We want to know in order to make ourselves free. That is our life: one universal cry for freedom.'

'Purity, patience, and perseverance are the three essentials to success, and above all- love.'

To the alienated youth from life, Swami Vivekananda inspires a positive attitude -

'What about this marvelous experience of standing alone, discarding all help, breasting the storms of life, of working without any sense of recompense, without any sense of putrid duty, and of working a whole life, joyful, free — not goaded on to work like slaves by false human love or ambition? Nature grinds all of us. Keep count of the ounce of pleasure you get. In the long run, nature

did her work through you, and when you die your body will make other plants grow. Yet, we think all the time that we are getting pleasure ourselves. Thus the wheel goes round.'

To the young atheists he imbibes the truth of ethereal existence.

'What do you gain in heaven? You become gods, drink nectar, and get rheumatism. There is less misery there than on earth, but also less truth...

You will be nearer to Heaven through football than through the study of the Gita.

I do not care for liberation (moksh); I would rather go to a hundred thousand hells, doing good to others (silently) like the spring- that is my religion.'

Swami Vivekananda believed that tradition as a 'value' gave identity and pride with a sense of belonging to a community and a nation, but he also found the prevalent social taboos, social stigmas, and social discriminations. He saw the socio-religious practices, rituals founded on superstitious beliefs and supernatural magic, socio cultural backwardness, illiteracy, poverty, conceited thoughts, and segregation of the women, as excrescencies detrimental to the progress of the society.

Superstition is our great enemy, but bigotry is worse.

The flaws were to be smoothened out by the young generation, not by a radical or fanatical revolution, but evolution of a rational open mind and a work culture of dedication and sincerity, without loss of the true essence of culture.

He is remembered as a youth inspiration for every generation. An eminent visionary educationist of eminence, a crusader for the alleviation of the socially and culturally backward, the unprivileged impoverished classes, the oppressed women and the ignorant segment of the society; but remembered most as a humanist.

His thoughts were moulded in ancient Indian ideals and virtues, synthesized with the western culture of humanism, science and technology; a unique culture to assimilate and inspire the youth with the spirit of freedom, equality, social economic justice, and respect for women, as necessity for Universal needs. It is most suited to our own contemporary eclectic society in the multicultural milieu, with the impact of globalization.

Vivekanandism is not a philosophical treatise, but a practical method to delve deep into the human emotions in the modern mechanistic grind, and understand the essence of life; and for every parent and educator to introspect and realize as conviction, that all life was endowed with divine natural elements, and that education alone could manifest that perfection in man in every moment of life. It was a rich repository of Universal inspirational heritage that was needed to be handed down as a legacy to the young generation, who have an important present, and a responsible future role to play towards themselves, their family, their community, their society, their nation and the world.

He found in the contemporary society, an admix of personalities - the orthodox and the liberal as actors in bipolar emotive levels of constant movements, either in a constraint of expression, or a retaliation in non acceptance of norms as conflicts- not in the class conflicts in the evolving society, but in personality conflicts by gender bias, social discrimination, social-cultural backwardness and wealth distribution, resulting in the social insecurity felt by each actor in the society.

The social movement experienced today is a similar distinct admix of personality conflicts of individuals, and the cultural admix with the impact of global trends, now accepted as a way of life. The occidental search for identity is now an oriental concern .

The inter generation lack of acceptance of each other's ideology is another problematic area in the increasing gap between the traditional conservative values, and liberal attitudes. The past fails to carry forward the conservative legacy, while the new generations will not accept it.

A child today learns in the changing global flux to develop a unique personality, which social scientists and psychologists fail to analyze correctly. In the metamorphose of an eclectic society, it becomes difficult to identify a personality trait, other than a social disorder or disability. It becomes difficult to understand our own generation today.

They, as players, fail to see the future or foresee the impediments they may face. With science and technology taking the centre stage, interestingly, some embrace it as a revolution, while others try to escape from it.

The trend is seen in the youth as immersive participation in their experiences, entertainment and expressions. They no longer want to passively watch. The shift to visual vocabulary and social media is the new trend in communication and expression, for the new generation.

It is the age of 'Impatience' in the constant demand for goods and services, with information flow that has accelerated expectation for 'instant' availability and success. This combination of impatience and impulsiveness keeps intensifying, often resulting in disappointments and frustrations. Ironically, the exposure to the experience of the unrealistic aspects of life, inspires both a huge surge, and an equally almost counter culture shunning it.

Parents can be assured that their fear by the onslaught of technology in the near future, will make the youth conscious of what they have lost in the unprecedented speed of change - and with time, will resent the mechanistic technological incursions. It is envisaged, they will gradually live in a more conscious way, shutting out distractions, and will focus on the moment most propitious from the inspirational guidance, to inculcate human values. Swami Vivekananda believed that it was not from academic books, but from the book of 'nature' and the knowledge about 'one self', that true education can be imparted.

'The book one must read to learn natural sciences is the book of nature. The book from which to learn religion is your own mind and heart.'

According to Swami Vivekananda: *'The education which does not help the common mass of people to equip themselves for the struggle of life, which does not bring out strength of character, spirit of philanthropy, and courage of a lion –is it worth the name? Education is that which character is formed, strength of mind is increased, the intellect is expanded, and by which one can stand on one's own feet.*'

This is both an individual and national endeavor, and consciousness of self reliance.

The basis of contemporary education however, is riddled with imperfections in flawed glory that reflects the human reality in the diversity of life as the poor qualitative texture of the society seen today, often polished and curated for social interactions in unapplied knowledge and wisdom, or in pseudo morality.

The disinterest in the children in learning for example, or understanding the disorder, is a challenge that parents and teachers face today, but unaware that they can find the solutions in the inspirations of Swami Vivekananda.

In a distorted unthinking adult world, the key to childhood, as Rabindranath Tagore reiterated are- 'creative spirit' and 'generous joy.' Unfortunately both are lost in the slew of academic policy changes, and marginalized in the mechanistic environment.

The element of compulsion, in the traditional pedagogy, has given way to the freedom of choice in rote learning or information assimilation from the digital technology for evolution of a 'mechanistic' mind, and in instant 'copy paste' culture or evaluation of performance through examinations that the youth dreads to face. They find easier means of escape in smug evasions. The creativity aspects that develop personality are ignored, and replaced by easy learning methods and entertainments that excite the animated behaviour in the comfort zone of complacency. Parents and social institutions, in order to give the best to a child, go overboard in their own helplessness, for easier path to success. They impose spirituality by rituals that has no meaning to a child, or information, as burdened imposed learning, that contributes no significance in the development of the child. We cannot ignore the flux in the society with easy access to information and technology to benefit the human race, but moderation and control is required as a corrective measure for the personality development of a child, else it will be difficult to understand our own children.

In our contemporary times, the relevance of Swami Vivekananda's '*inspirations*' for the youth towards '*self reliance*' and '*positive thinking*' are simple illuminating concepts of confidence, determination and courage to proclaim –

'*if you think yourself strong, strong will you be. With weakness comes ignorance, and with ignorance comes misery.*'

Purity of heart with no hate for others, to respect the dignity of life with humility, patience, perseverance are some of the essentials to success.

The National Policy on Education (1986) outlined a child centered system of education as departure from structured learning to pursue imaginative activities so as to inculcate creativity with opportunities for contemplation, freedom and generate new knowledge with other resources as participants in learning. If learning is to be restructured and reoriented then a 'motivational' inspiration can help a child to realize his experience as an 'experiment with reality'. Thoughts were moulded in Swami Vivekananda's own experience by observations in the deviations in the socio cultural environment of his times as a process of learning. He searched the ancient scriptures and literature to determine the human essence: *to excite the marginalized emotional intelligence and ignite the rational mind.*

The aim of the present series of parables as *Inspirations from Swami Vivekananda: Parables for Young Readers* is to offer the emotive motivational inspirations, from some of the basic teachings and thoughts of Swami Vivekananda to the young children of every social domain and nationality, as instructive principles; to illustrate '*values*' in day to day life in children as inferential learning, for self realization in participatory experiences, with positive thinking that needs to be imbibed in the new generation, as a new paradigm for success that has Universal appeal.

The real '*Moksha*' according to Swami Vivekananda comes not in individuals from alienation, hermitage or surrender of life, but from striving for a better life in participatory amelioration of the masses; not through petty politics of human confrontation or revolution, but evolution of the human self, through physical, intellectual and spiritual excellence, as integral to the value dimensions inherent and endowed by 'Nature', in the indomitable and '*never say die*' spirit of man. He inspires the youth to work hard with perseverance, and a determined will for success:

'To Succeed, you must have tremendous perseverance, tremendous will: 'I will drink the ocean', says the preserving soul, 'at my will, mountains will

crumble up.' Have that sort of energy, that sort of will, work hard, and you will reach the goal!'

Swami Vivekananda inspires the youth in his words:

'My faith is in younger generation, the modern generation. They will work out the problems like lions. Do not look back upon what has been done. Go ahead!'

The four stories – *Restless Shadows, Naren, Tantric Baba* and Beleh are parables of Swami Vivekananda's inspirational essence for the young readers that will arouse the latent emotional intelligence and ignite the young mind to a more purposeful meaning of life, specially in the formative age of 13+ in the development of the explorative rational mind of our young readers.

THE RESTLESS SHADOWS

'Knowledge can be got only through one way, the way of experience; there is no other way to know.'

- Swami Vivekananda

THE RESTLESS SHADOWS

In ancient times, the river *Saraswati* flowed from the lofty Himalayan mountains, down the lush green valley, *meandering* slowly like a *glistening* snake, through numerous forests with vast *biodiversity* of *flora* and *fauna*.

It was a time of *abundance* for everyone to share the *bounties* of nature. Travellers, pilgrims or the king's soldiers would rest under the shade of trees, and feast on the fresh fruits, nuts and honey from the forest. Saints would meditate under the shade of trees, in peace and tranquility. The clear cool river would *quench* their thirst. The soft wind, blowing through the forest that whistled in *symphony* with the melodious chirping birds, would evoke a feeling of joy. The melody of the forest and the fragrance of the flowers, would spread across the forest. It would be a refreshing delight to listen to the music of nature. The fluttering colorful butterflies would be a joyful sight.

Such was the beauty of nature.

During those days, the banks of a river offered an ideal peaceful place, away from bustling towns and cities for Rishis to set up their Ashrams, or Gurukul schools. The Rishis were both revered and feared, for they were men of wisdom, and also trained in marshal arts. Some

Rishis had acquired magical powers. They could conjure up frightening images to keep wild beasts and evil people at bay. The Rishis could cast a spell or a curse if they were displeased, or angered.

A few Rishis were ascetics. They were calm and composed, and often lived alone in hermitage, with vow of celibacy and austerity; while others had a family with children. Some of the famous Rishi Gurukuls were much sought after by young disciples, who came from near and far off kingdoms.

In ancient times, there were no boarding schools. A Gurukul under a Rishi was the only place, where young princes and children from noble families went to learn the basics of Vedic literature, and also hone skills in marshal arts. However, not all were taken in. Only the best students were accepted in the Gurukul, if they were found suitable and keen to learn, by the learned Rishi.

The Rishis in Ashrams were stern and disciplined; but they were also kind, and allowed the children to play and learn in the natural surroundings near the Ashram.

Learning was fun.

The young children had ample time to themselves. They played and made friends. The classes were very interesting, as the Rishis narrated ancient tales to them. The children were free to do whatever they best liked.

Everyone in the Ashram, from a prince to a common student, was treated equally with equal share of work. Each student had the freedom to express freely, although no one could complain of any difficult task given, even if he was the son of a great king.

The little children however, away from their homes had freedom to play, while the elder boys had a more tedious task of learning scriptures and the art of weapons, or performing Ashram duties. There was absolute faith and a bond between the Rishi and his disciples. There was brotherly love amongst the children.

In one such ashram, Rishi Devbrat devoted his entire life in imparting education to his students. Most of his disciples had been famous kings and men of wisdom. As a tradition, the kings sent their wards to the Ashram at a very young age. The Rishi's wife, Guruma would look after the young children like a caring mother.

Among his young students was a four year old precocious child, Satyabrat- the crown prince of a nearby kingdom.

In the environ of lush green nature, life in 'Gurukul' was a serene vibrant time for the frolicking children - away from all the worldly cares- away from the pomp of palace life. There, the children lived like brothers; the Rishi and the Guruma were like parents.

The Ashram was a wonderful place to stay with love, care and understanding as a family. There were many things for the curious little children to learn for themselves. It was exciting to find the hidden treasures of nature. The natural surroundings had many mysteries to solve.

The bird's nest with little eggs, the colorful fish swimming gracefully in the clear river, the beehive that dripped golden honey, the tasty ripe fruits up the trees, the fluttering colorful butterflies, the incessant melody of the song birds, were delightful experiences for the little children from the distant towns and palaces.

The flippant life of the children, slowly changed to a sober one, in the somber tranquil environment around.

The peaceful starlit nights with the silver moon casting long shadows of the forest trees, offered new adventures in exciting thrill. Although the little children were not permitted to go out in the forest, they would watch and listen to the haunting nocturnal sounds. Wild beasts and frightening shadowy apparitions, moved freely in the dark night!

'Why do we fear shadows at night, and not by day?'

quipped Satyabrat one evening, when the children had gathered to listen to a story the Rishi narrated. Each night, it was a different story of far off places - about valour, hard work, good spirits or the evil spirits in this world.

'Evil begets evil', said the Rishi in a solemn tone. *'Goodness begets the light of knowledge. All the evil spirits that manifest in this world are mere dark shadows that loom in our mind to frighten us. It is this fear that you must conquer!'*

The young children huddled together as the Rishi related a story of an evil witch who had cast a spell on a kingdom, and how a brave prince outwitted her, to finally imprison her.

'Do we also need magic to capture the evil spirits?' asked a curious child who had been listening intently.

'Yes, my child', said the Rishi. *'Light of knowledge is the magic that dispels the dark evil fear. You will learn the 'mantras' that can keep the evil spirit away that roam the forests and towns without rest, to frighten people. The mantras will help you to be fearless.'*

The elder boys were fearless, as the Rishi had taught them 'mantras' to protect themselves and others. The little children too, one day would learn, to be courageous and fearless, as they grew up.

Like most curious small children, Satyabrat was also curious. He was keen to learn the mysteries of nature. He would get up at night to listen to the hoot of the owl, or the chatter of some disturbed nocturnal bird. He knew that the evil fear of the dark would rest in the day.

At the break of dawn, he would sit on the threshold

of the hut to watch the red glow of the rising sun.

One morning, when the Rishi was going to the river for his morning holy ablutions, Sayabrat quickly joined his teacher.

'Guruji, why does the sun go away at night? Why is it dark at night?' Satyabrat questioned, looking up at his teacher.

The wise Rishi replied tenderly, holding the child's hand.

'My child. The bright sun does not go away. Just as you go behind the hut to play hide and seek with your friends, and are not seen, the sun also goes behind our great planet.'

The Rishi gave simple examples to clear every shadow of doubt in the child's inquisitive mind. Satyabrat listened in awe as they reached the river bank.

'Just as the oil lamp we light at night, dispels darkness, the sun too is a huge source of energy that gives heat and light, to dispel the night.'

Satyabrat then thanked his Guru and scampered away to play with his friends. When the morning fun was over, the young lad sought something new to ask his Guru the next day. This was how Sayabrat learnt the many mysteries of nature.

One morning, when Satyabrat was sitting beside a tree, pondering over what his guru had explained about

the sun and darkness, his attention was drawn to the shadow of the tree, which inched slowly on the ground. It inched longer and longer, as the day grew brighter, with the rising morning sun.

Satyabrat pondered for a moment.

'Well I have no fear of this shadow. It must be a good spirit.'

Yet, there was something puzzling that nagged his young mind.

'Was the tree growing larger?'

He looked at the tree.

'No, it had not grown tall.'

Some inner impulse prompted him to stand up. He saw his own thin shadow fall on the ground. It was also growing larger every minute with the rising sun.

'Am I growing tall? No, it can't be so. My legs and arms are still the same - so is the tree. Yet, my shadow grows taller like the shadow of the tree every moment.'

He was puzzled.

Satyabrat bent down to touch his shadow. To his surprise, the shadow just shrunk towards him, and disappeared!

As he straightened up, the shadow reappeared to stretch on the ground.

It was like magic to him!

'Let me just catch you!' muttered Satyabrat. He took a step forward, and the shadow stretched a step. He stamped on the shadow, and the shadow jumped a step further. He leaped forward, so did the shadow. Satyabrat then turned around to find that the shadow was still behind him!

'I'll get you!'

He charged towards the shadow. He did not give up. He twisted and turned, ran round and round, walked to and fro to throw the shadow away, but alas! The shadow would not part from him. It followed him stubbornly.

The Ashram boys around were amused to see Satyabrat rushing madly at his own shadow. They had gathered to see his comic act. His movements were ridiculous and funny. Their giggling became laughter, and then a roar of hilarious boisterous shouting!

All work at Ashram came to a standstill. Even *Guruma* came out to see the commotion. They were all amused to watch the funny antics of Satyabrat. The somber silent Ashram had become a lively place.

Satyabrat felt a deep sense of shame and ignominy, when he saw everyone watching his funny show. He ran behind the tree, hid behind the huge trunk, and stood crest fallen. He had made a clown of himself. Such funny antics by young children were common in the Ashram. Chasing a shadow now became a new exciting game for them. Every young child joined the fun.

For Satyabrat, it was a search to know the truth. The young child mused at the problem, but found no answer. He became a little awry, and finally went to his Guru.

Rishi Devbrat was not busy. He beckoned the child to come forward.

Satyabrat's face brightened up.

'My child', explained the wise Rishi. *'The shadow that you see is your own when your body blocks light. When the trees block the sun's light, the shadow stretches longer and longer with the rising sun'*

Truth dawned on Satyabrat. He stood listening agape.

'Knowledge of Truth is the bright light that dispels all shadow of ignorance, fear and doubt', continued the wise Rishi very patiently. *'Your search to know has given you knowledge; and joy to your friends.'*

Satyabrat was one of the best disciples of Rishi Devbrat. After his education in the Ashram, and with the Guru's blessings, Satyabrat became a wise king in the kingdom. He was known for his honesty and dedication to work.

The running shadows of ignorance, doubt and fear had vanished from his mind.

*

Delusion will vanish as the light becomes more and more effulgent, load after load of ignorance will vanish, and then will come a time when all else has disappeared and the sun alone shines.

- Swami Vivekananda

NAREN

Take up an idea.
Make that one idea your life - think of it,
dream of it, and live on idea.
Let the brain, muscles, nerves,
every part of your body,
be full of that idea, and just leave
every other idea alone.
This is the way to success.
Condemn none: if you can stretch out a helping hand, do so. If you cannot, fold your hands, bless your brothers, and let them go their own way.

- Swami Vivekananda

NAREN

Naren was sad.

The roll of the distant thunder announced the departure of the rains, leaving a musty dampness of silent desolation. The water droplets dripped in a rhythmic '*plop*' sound, from the soggy thatched roof, complaining like a leaky faucet, wanting repair.

The rains had flooded the mud hut with few pots afloat. They were the only possession the family had. The young boy, helplessly waded in the water to salvage the pots, which like some paper boat adrift, swayed aimlessly to the open threshold. The soggy bamboo frame door, hung limp with no props. The damp mud wall could not support it. The dark trees beyond, filtered dim grey light of hopelessness. The air was humid with an eerie quietness.

The tropical monsoon rain had swept clean the dark green foliage around, to glisten in a dull hue. The insects, like the homeless refugees from the east, had crawled out from their flooded holes. The dark ravens perched speechless, shivering wet on the nearby *Neem* tree, were like undertakers to a funeral. The rain gods gave no succour to the dark wetland, growing profuse weeds in village *Bagnan*, nor did the human gods care for the weeds. The *Nawab was* the human god who ruled the beggarly lot, and the weeds in the sorrowful land of Bengal.

Naren, a poor Brahmin lad of seven, lived in the dilapidated mud hut in the impoverished village. There were no schools or teachers to tutor the young lad. He had no companions, save his own self, to share his joy and despondence.

Padmavati, his old widowed mother, was his only family. She was left alone with her child. Sorrow had struck a few months ago in their derisory life. The boy had lost his brothers and sisters, a few days before his seventh birthday. They had been carried away with their father, in the swollen fury of the *Damodar River*, never to be found again.

It was their last holy rite in the river of sorrow. Pundit Ashutosh Mukhopadhya, the *Kuleen Brahmin* had performed it joyfully on land.

Naren's *'Upanayana'* ceremony, on his coming of age was abandoned. He was the last of the eleven joyful sorrows; a winsome lad, who never complained to gods or humans for his sorrows and pain.

The desolate village had a few families remaining. Some were the untouchable miserable on the outskirts of the village, surviving on menial work, plodding in the murky paddy field with their naked children; while the rich landlords sent their children to Pundit Ashutosh Mukhopadhya, to be trained as uncivil Zamindars.

Naren was a Brahmin, yet to be initiated into the new learning of *'Brahamalogy'*.

He was born in a caste, sanctified in the scriptures

by the zealot practitioners of orthodoxy, to lead a life of misery, living in penury on the offerings to the dead, or to the gods, with vows of indebtedness.

The three strands in the sacred thread; a constant reminder of purity in one's mind, words and deeds.

They were the impoverished lot, living on charity of those superstitious 'souls', who wanted freedom for their dear departed, or to cleanse their abode from the evil spirit, that brought ill luck.

Neither luck, nor did the gods favor the lonesome dual souls. The meager handful of rice his mother brought home, knotted at one corner of her coarse cotton white sari, from someone with mercy, could not satiate the persistent pangs of hunger.

They suppressed their hunger, gulping tumbler full water, like stranded fish on land gulping air, torturously flopping on the ground to survive; or with some impulsive surge one day, flip into the ethereal space, to gracefully glide away to a second life.

Padmavati wanted to survive; so did Naren. Despite the misfortunes and the bleak future, Padmavati felt, her son Naren, a Brahmin by birth should receive the grace of goddess Saraswati, to continue the tradition of work. Learning the Holy Scriptures by rote was the only source of livelihood for the Brahmins. It would be Naren's fortune and future. He would be blessed by the goddess of prosperity, if Pundit Ashutosh Mukhopadya accepted the child in his fold, as a disciple; the 'Upanayana' ceremony performed by a *'Kuleen Brahmin'* would be a propitious auspicious moment.

The Brahmin temerity that flowed in her blood, urged

the ardent heart to take the hopeful pilgrimage. She performed her daily rituals of prayers and fasting for the fortunate day.

At the break of day, she set off with Naren, across the forest to the other end of the village. Here lived the learned Pundit in the temple of the venerated goddess Kali, feared for her feminine vengeance on male demons.

The dark forest of *Bagnan* was a fearful place for young children to wander. The wandering souls of the cremated dead, near the river were reported by the villagers, to scream at night, pleading for liberty.

All heard, but none helped.

The repeated chanting of '*Shiva*' would ward off the evil spirits. Mother and son quickened their pace, whispering the holy word, to keep the sleeping souls undisturbed, in the rising dull day.

In twenty minutes, they were in the open fields. The distant temple bells, clangoured to beckon the pilgrims, and worship the fearful goddess. It was another festive day for the superstitious many. It was another favourable day for hungry village dogs and beggarly humans to share some morsel.

The frail women with her child, painfully stepped up the temple stairs to the goddess, and prayed.

The temple was visited by the gullible rustics from the villagers around. It was an auspicious day. The few early devotees soon grew into a serpentine queue. They had offerings for the goddess who never ate. The major portion was taken away by the disciples in baskets for the high priest; the crumbs leftover for the temple rats.

The hungry two, sat near the temple stairs for the

human offerings. The handful of morsel from each devotee that holy day, was plenty to fill the shrunken stomach for a few days. Padmavati seldom came here with her son. The extra *'prasad'* she received, was carefully wrapped in the small linen cloth she had brought along. It was to be their morsel, for the next day.

When the temple doors closed for the goddess to rest, it was past noon. Padmavati and Naren hurriedly got up to meet Pundit Ashutosh Mukhopadhya, before he sat down for his holy ritual of sharing the day's offerings to the gods, and himself. Later, he would take his routine undisturbed noon siesta till late evening. It was forbidden to meet him then. The gods and priests rested, while the students learned scriptures in the humid noon.

Mother and son hurried to the rear of the temple, where the *'Kuleen Brahmin'* resided.

They found the obese dark man, standing arms akimbo, surveying the basketful of offerings on the floor brought in by his disciples. He was clad in *'a soiled kurta and dhoti'*. There was a dull aura of a demanding domineering obedience in his posture. A placid menacing demeanor writ on his visage; his eyes gleaming in satisfied panache that the villagers feared the goddess, and the high priest - Pundit Ashutosh Mukhopadhya.

Pundit Ashutosh Mukhopadhya was a *'Kuleen'* priest. A lineage of the highest pure order from the ancient past. They had the social sanction, to absolve the social stigma of child widowhood, by matrimonial alliance. He was the lord of the poor widows - a savior, who had saved many a helpless soul to find a place in hell or heaven.

The condemned helpless young widows, ostracized from villages and nearby towns, were led to his humble dwellings, but after agreeing to an assured sum from the pleading fathers as dowry, to redeem them in nuptial ties.

The first five marriages were never consummated. They all had found *'liberty'* from the matrimonial bondage in illness. The last widow he had married, unfortunately jumped into the well and drowned.

The pundit looked up from the *'worldly'* offerings, to the 'spiritual' hope of redemption in another matrimonial alliance, when he saw Padmavati, clad in a white coarse cotton sari, step up to prostrate in obeisance to the *'Kuleen Brahmin'*.

He recognized her immediately with a suppressed smile. He had arranged the holy rituals, a few months back, for the departed souls of her family to rest in peace. He had directed the villagers and the landlords to pool in the *'resources'* for the *'final rituals'* and the village *'feast'*, for the holy dead. The offerings were plenty for the gods, and the high priest.

He was sympathetic to the young widow: Her indebtedness perpetual.

'It is good to see you', he said in a mild tone. *'What brings you here?'*

Even before the widow could utter a word, Pundit Mukhopadhya noticed the young boy. *'Ah, I see you have brought your young son along. Well son, have you started to learn the Holy Scriptures?'*

Padmavati found it expedient moment to cut in.

'It is exactly why I have come to meet you. I would

be much obliged if you take my son as your disciple. As a Brahmin, he would make a good student and a priest. His 'Upanayana' thread ceremony is yet to be solemnized.'

'Oh!' Pundit Mukhopadhya's face lit up in surprise, and then faded to a sullen thought. He was both surprised and disappointed. He remained silent. This was unexpected!

He mused thoughtfully. *'If I agree, it'll give me opportunity to meet the young lady often. Perhaps in near future, seek her hand. The young boy too, would be helpful as a disciple in the temple work.'*

'Alright', he said sternly in affirmation. *'Send him everyday before dawn. I will have the thread ceremony performed tomorrow. He will learn the 'Sandya-vandanum' scriptures till evening and return home. I have no extra room for the child. He may take meals in the temple with other students'.*

His non-chalant reply was like the direction he gave to his minions.

He did not want the widow to know the tiny core of compassion he had for her. He looked at her with a grim smile. She would, forever be indebted and servile to him for his generosity. She would succumb to his indebtedness one day. The male chauvinist pandit stood silent, awaiting her response.

'Punditji, I am highly obliged', she answered, with both palms pressed in gratitude. *'You do not know how relieved I am. I do not know how to 'repay' you. God will definitely reward you for your kindness someday.'*

Pundit Mukhopadhya felt elated with the praise. His

hope rekindled with the word *'repay'* the widow had assured. *'It would take a few months for the young widow to accept his proposal'* he thought impatiently - *'or, he could send word through the priest in the next village with the matrimonial proposal direct to the widow. She would not turn down such a good offer.'*

He gloated with happiness at his plan.

That night, he was restless in his thoughts of the seventh marriage vow he would solemnize. He would calculate the most auspicious favorable day for the marriage soon. The villagers would arrange everything for the *'Kuleen Brahmin'* wedding. It would be the talk around many villages with his praises *–the savior of the young helpless Brahmin widow! He soon dozed off to his world of fantasy.*

Naren had already made friends with some of the young students at the temple. When he related about the broken down hut where he stayed, his new friends were touched with compassion. Some boys collected a bundle of dry grass stored in the rear temple room and offered it to Naren. He was overwhelmed with joy, for the love and care they shared with him.

Mother and son returned home with the bundle of grass. The flooded room had drained out, but the floor was still damp. The dry grass made a comfortable dry bed. They slept well in the melodious night, with the frogs croaking and the crickets serenading.

The next morning, Naren was up early for the ritual ablutions. The young child was excited to meet his new friends.

'Listen to Punditji during the learning session. You

must always respect your Guruji', told her mother. She also warned him not to play truant, and to return home before the dark.

'I will, dear mother', replied Naren. He set off to go to his new temple school. He was in a happy mood. However, when he entered the dark forest, his little heart began to beat quickly in fear. He expected the evil spirits to emerge any moment. He quickened his walk to a scamper. He ran along the dirt track and was breathless when he reached the temple. The sight of the temple and the young students brightened him up.

He soon forgot about the forest spirits.

He paid his respect to his teacher by touching his feet. He was next prepared for the *'Upanayana'* thread rituals. The rites began amidst chanting of the scriptures, while one priest began shaving Naren's curly hair. The sacred thread marked his transition to a second birth to knowledge.

It was a crucial event in the life of every orthodox Hindu, with vow of celibacy and indebtedness to the ancestors, to the sages who had endowed the next generation with the knowledge of the Veda, and to the teacher who imparted it.

Naren was a keen learner. He had already learnt the first ten verses on the first day during the second meditation *sandhyavandanum* session. Pundit Mukhopadhya was a stern teacher. He did not like his disciples to chant verses with flaw.

The young monks, donning the priestly attire sat down in a row for the noon meals served on banana leaves. The noon meal cooked by the elder students for the special occasion was simple, but sumptuous. Apart from learning, the young children loved the temple meals. They came to know each other intimately during the break.

'Do you not fear walking through the forest?' enquired Naren from a boy who also came through the forest from a nearby village.

'Yes. But I feel secure because my brother escorts me everyday', replied the young child. Naren sighed with want of care. He wished someone would also accompany him in his lonely eerie walk through the forest.

That night, Naren asked his mother if she could accompany him each day.

'Alas my child, I have to go out to collect alms from different homes to keep us going. We cannot afford a servant, nor can I come with you, we will not be able to survive,' she said sadly.

She was a pious lady and had faith in her lord Krishna.

'When you go through the forest, call out to the young cowherd Krishna. He'll come to you as a brother, and accompany you', his mother assured him. Naren was baffled. He had never heard of any cowherd named Krishna in the village!

Naren went through the forest next day and called out, *'Brother Krishna, brother Krishna, where are you?'*

There was no reply. Then, after a brief silence, he heard the distant mooing of cattle. The cows soon emerged from the forest, with metal bells clanging around their neck. They stopped near Naren. Behind them appeared a small child cowherd.

'Are you calling me?' He enquired gently.

'Yes', Naren replied.

His mother had told him the truth. There was really a cowherd Krishna. He was happy and excited to find another boy of his own age as his companion. Krishna escorted Naren through the forest. They talked like intimate friends.

'Do you live in the forest?' asked Naren one day. He was amazed, because he had never seen or heard of the boy cowherd before, although his mother knew about him!

'I live everywhere', said Krishna with a smile. *'I am happy that you now go to the temple to study scriptures.*

I have seen you often in the village, but you failed to see me.'

Krishna and Naren shared their talk like brothers. The bond of friendship was strong. The years rolled past. Naren now knew the scriptures, and was ready to perform the duties of a holy priest.

However, on the day of completion, every student was indebted to the teacher. They had to offer '*Guru Dakshina*', as repayment of their debt to Pundit Mukhopadhya. It was a day of rituals and feast. Every student planned to give the best gift. Some thought of presenting the 'fresh' honey of the season, while others gave money or hand woven cloth.

Poor Naren was sad. He had nothing to offer.

'What shall I do?' he asked his mother helplessly.

'Why don't you ask brother Krishna?' replied his mother. *'He'll have something to offer.'*

So the next day, Naren called out to Krishna in the forest. As usual, Krishna appeared - *'Yes brother Naren, you called me?'*

'Brother Krishna, I am too poor to give anything to my teacher as 'Guru Dakshina' on the last day of my studies. Some zamindar children mock at my poverty,' said Naren.

'Don't worry. Here - take this pitcher of milk', Krishna said, handing Naren a small old brass pitcher. *'I'm sure your teacher, if worthy of this gift, will appreciate the richness of the milk'*.

Naren was happy. He clutched the small pitcher in his hands and went to the temple.

When he reached the temple, the young children had already laid their gifts in front of Pundit Mukhopadhya. The teacher sat under the shade of a *Peepal* tree, receiving the gifts gleefully, and then blessing the students.

When it was Naren's turn, a frown of disapproval came across Pundit Mukhopadhya's visage, when he saw the small old pitcher.

'What is this you bring to me?' asked his teacher grimly. He expected every student to bring gifts of value. A small old pitcher with milk was worthless to him!

'Give it to the temple servant', Pundit Mukhopadhya sneered with contempt for the child, and the gift.

Naren felt a deep sense of shame. The rich boys laughed when the servant took the pitcher away. The rituals continued with other boys bringing gifts. Some had brought baskets full of fruits, rice, sweets and other goodies for the guru.

Naren stood silent.

The ceremony suddenly broke into a commotion and shouting when the temple servant came running, bewildered with astonishing news.

'Guruji!' he exclaimed in utter surprise. *'This pitcher fills up again when it is emptied.'*

'How can it be possible?' said Pundit Mukhopadhya doubtfully. *'Let me see it.'*

He looked at the ordinary old pitcher carefully. He then emptied the milk in another container. *Lo! The pitcher began to fill up again!*

'This is amazing!' declared Pundit Mukhopadhya, not willing to believe his eyes. The other boys stared in bewilderment.

'This is witchcraft magic. It is 'Maya'. Who gave you this pitcher?' he asked the silent boy.

'My friend Krishna, the cowherd gave it to me', replied Naren truthfully. *'He lives in the forest.'*

'Forest indeed! You are a liar!' the Pundit snorted. *'There is no such cowherd named Krishna in this village or forest. Only the evil spirits live there!'*

'It is true Punditji. If you come along with me in the forest, I'll call him to meet you'. Naren offered, to prove his innocence.

The entire ignorant people from the temple trudged in bewildered fear following Naren in the forest. They reached the forest and stood silently for Naren to call the boy cowherd.

'Brother Krishna, brother Krishna come out to meet Pundit ji.' Naren called. *'He does not believe you gave me the magic pitcher.'*

Poor Naren called out repeatedly in earnest for a long time.

No Krishna appeared.

The *'Kuleen Brahmin'* left the forest in a huff throwing down the pitcher, followed by the retinue of his disciple, cursing the young boy for befooling them with *a magic pitcher, given by some evil spirit*!

Naren was left alone crying. They had called him a liar and unfit to be a priest.

'Krishna, you have failed me!' sobbed Naren. He felt miserable.

'Brother Naren!' A distant soft voice echoed in the forest. *'I have not failed you. The pundit does not deserve the gift, because he has no faith. He is greedy. I come to people who are pure in heart. The pitcher is your gift from me to feed the hungry. It is now time for you to go out to the world to enlighten the ignorant. To teach love and faith to all. If you have belief to overcome obstacles in life, you will never fail.'*

Naren was ordained a true priest, to perform his humble duty as a savior of humanity by courage and endurance, to face both the miseries and happiness of life.

*

The disciple must have great power of endurance. Life seems comfortable; and you find the mind behaves well when everything is going well with you. But if something goes wrong, your mind loses its balance. That is not good. Bear all evil and misery without one murmur of hurt, without one thought of unhappiness, resistance, remedy, or retaliation. That is true endurance; and that you must acquire.

- Swami Vivekananda

THE TANTRIC BABA

The moment you fear, you are nobody. It is fear that is the greatest cause of misery in the world. It is fear that is the greatest of all superstitions. It is fear that is the cause of our woes, and it is fearlessness that brings heaven in a moment.

- Swami Vivekananda

THE TANTRIC BABA

The dark Shivpur village lay sprawled damp in the humid monsoon. The flooded paddy fields of Shivpur, stretched to the distant murky *Damodar River* that swirled in fury, and inundated the villages beyond. It was like a huge wild anaconda on a rampage, swallowing anything that came its way.

The ignorant rustics had appeased the river god in vain. The ritual offerings on the river bank had been swept away with the decrepit homes and the starving animals. The sparse harvest had wilted.

It was the sorrow of south Bengal.

The *'Kalbaishak'* monsoon had drenched the parched land. The days of famine were over; the unfortunate survivors would however, die in pestilence. Disease and illness would take its toll. The gods were deaf to the wailing souls : Voodooism would hear them : Fear would rule in the hearts and mind of the villagers.

The superstitious villagers sent for the wizen *'Tantric Baba'!*

He did not arrive.

The helpless Shivpur village, patiently limped back to the sowing season. The *emaciated* villagers toiled in shrunken hope, with their *jejune* children as co-workers till dusk. Some scrawny ones, stayed home to help their sanforized mothers. A few *gaunt* fortunate, played '*pithu*' in the courtyard, while the little *skeletal* infants lay swaying in bamboo cradles.

Srilata, a fortune survivor of female feticide was a non believer in '*spirits*'. Her father Ramakanto, the poor solitary village '*druid*' collected medicinal herbs for a living. His small family prepared herbal 'round pills' for ailments of every kind. It was later sold in the weekend '*Hatt*'. He earned just enough to keep his family of three alive.

He left no inheritance to them when he died two years ago, from an ailing heart. His young daughter Srilata, had to visit the distant town of Madhavpur, for her father's ailment. The doctor in the dispensary had instructed her, about the dangers of a weak heart, before the unfortunate demise of her father. On the sad day, during the sudden heart seizure, she had desperately tried to revive him, but in vain.

The family was left with nothing, but misery and poverty.

It was Srilata, who now continued her father's legacy. She was a young girl of thirteen years; her childhood usurped by sadness.

Aunt Savita and her young son Sunder from the neighboring hut, often came over to help the family. Srilata made the herbal pills by collecting the herbs from the nearby forest. In addition, she collected marigold flowers that grew in abundance near the river banks and in the periphery of the forests, to make garlands for the devotees, who thronged the village *'Bhairav'* temple, during auspicious days. It supplemented the family meager income.

She was helped by her old widowed mother, and her young brother, Bolu.

Bolu was a scraggy child, aged nine.

It was always fun for the little children, to burst out from their homes to play like runaway peas from a pod. Even when the monsoon rain pelted down suddenly, the young children pranced joyfully, till they were drenched and called in by their mothers.

It was one evening in the month of *'Greeshm'*, when the summer heat lingered till midnight, that a sudden pall descended on Shivpur. The lively evening for the children turned to a sudden hush. The skylight suddenly seemed to fade to a grayish darkness. Bolu and his friends, hurriedly abandoned their *'pithu'* game. The stack of seven stone *'pithu'* toppled over, like some crumbling tower, as the children left in haste.

It was the ominous dull thumping of a resounding dilapidated drum, through the forest path, that brought a cold chill terror in the young children. They froze momentarily.

The long drawn blast from the conch, announced the arrival of the dreaded *'Tantric Baba'* in the village. He had come to rid the village of the evil spirits!

The dirt track was cleared for the fearful *'Tantric Baba'*. The village bore a desolate calm. It was now deserted.

The pariah village dogs howled the ominous arrival.

The young children dared not face the magic

medicine man in fear. They felt annoyed with their play ruined, and now would be ushered in their homes, by their mothers.

Whenever the 'Baba' arrived in the village, a fearful hush descended in the twilight. He had come to drive away some hounding evil spirit, lurking in some household, or a ghost from the darkness at night in the 'Neem' tree, from where it frightened the villagers. Young children were forbidden to go near the tree in the dusk. The evil spirit could harm them.

A family with sickness or bad luck would often invite the 'Baba', to drive away the spirit. He would, with his magical incantations challenge the 'spirit' during the rituals. The 'spirit' would then enter the body of a child, and flee at the *Baba's* command. The villagers offered money and gifts to the *Baba* for the rituals. They dreaded the *Baba,* for he could spell out a curse, if displeased.

The previous year, Ramulu's sick daughter had become hysterical during the rituals. She swayed her head like some lunatic possessed by evil spirit. She twisted and turned in torturous convulsions, like a captured wild beast, struggling desperately to get free. Some womenfolk had to pin her down to the ground. It was amazing to see how a weak girl could possess so much strength. She was beaten with a broom by the *'Baba'* to drive out the evil spirit in her. She then swayed from side to side in a swoon, and finally became suddenly limp. She was carried away home to sleep, with the evil spirit fleeing. Unfortunately, she was not cured. She died a few months later in her illness.

The superstitious rustics thought otherwise.

The fear of the evil spirit and the *'Baba'* persisted in the villagers. The *'Baba'* was displeased. The girl had died mysteriously as the *'Baba'* had used magic spells

directed to Ramulu, the poor peasant. The miserable man had nothing to offer for the *'tantric'* session.

'Who do you think has called the dreaded man to our village?' asked Shamu, turning around as he went home, his shrunken hollow eyes in terror.

'I don't know.....I'm going home', replied Bolu nervously. He would know about the visit when he reached home. He walked briskly to find his nervous mother waiting at the door, her face pale in anxiety.

The dark shadow of fear had descended to eclipse the entire village.

'Come in quickly, Bolu', she said, hustling the child inside. She slammed the door shut, and quickly fastened the door latch. The other members of the family were all there.

Bolu's elder sister Srilata, cousin Sunder and aunt Savita sat huddled together in one corner of the room on the floor. The strong smell of marigold flower came across the small room. In the middle was a pile of golden yellow marigold flowers. They were all threading flowers to make garlands to sell to the villagers for the evening rituals. They would do brisk business that evening.

Bolu joined in to help.

The sudden clanking of the iron shackles on the door was a momentary break from their laborious task.

'Who could it be?' enquired Bolu's mother, looking up from her work. She went to the door and opened it.

Shamu, Bolu's friend stood on the threshold with his mother.

'Do you mind if Shamu stays till the evening rituals are over? She asked.

'Sure', replied Bolu's mother. *'He can stay. The children will remain at home and play together'*. She ushered Shamu in the room, while his mother hurried off.

Shamu shuffled across uneasily, and sat down with the others. *'What does this Baba do? Why is everyone in the village frightened?'* asked Shamu out of fearful curiosity.

'Now remember one thing children', aunt Savita told sternly, first glancing at her son Sunder, and then at Shamu. *'You are not to ask questions about the tantric Baba!'*

'He's just a magic man who uses magic to ward off evil', added Srilata. She noticed a glint of excitement in Bolu's eyes.

'Now children, remember one thing! Don't dare to go near the Baba when he performs the magic. The evil spirit may get hold of you!' Aunt Savita warned, looking at her son Sunder. *'Only the adults in the village are permitted to attend. You all are to stay here till the rituals are over!'*

There was a sudden hush in the room. The children were, in their own mood with thoughts of mischief, although busily threading the flowers. They could read one another's mind.

With their work completed, the small group sat down to play a new game that Srilata had invented- *'Find the Saint.'*

It was a simple game. Slips were distributed. The unfortunate one with a slip marked 'Devil' was to find out the 'saint' who would begin some animated action that everyone mimicked. The game was a hilarious one!

Aunt Savita and Srilata's mother had left with the flowers to sell before the rituals began.

Time flew away like the tired evening birds to their roosting nests. The redness in the sky began to mellow, and finally to a silent darkness. The echoing sound of the conch beckoned the villagers to the magic of the Tantric Baba.

The children in the room soon grew tired of their game. They were restless. They wanted a new adventure!

'Let's go and see what the villagers are doing?' suggested Bolu. *'It would be real fun to watch them perform the rituals!'*

'No!' , warned Shamu. *'Remember what your aunt Savita told us?'*

'Coward! I know you are afraid,' Bholu said vehemently. He liked to tease Shamu.

'Not in the least. I dare you to join me to see the rituals', challenged Shamu, more out of arrogance than his fear.

Srilata had been silent. She was amused by the dauntless challenges of the boys. In fact,she herself wanted to see what the magic rituals were like.

'Let's all go', she suggested. *'But mind you, never to be seen by anyone, else we would be in real trouble!'*

The children huddled to confer together in hushed voices. They made plans for the evening adventure.

'We'll keep some distance away and hide ourselves', Bholu said excitedly. *'We'll cover our faces with scarves!'* added Sunder.

'We are not bandits', Srilata laughed. *'No one will notice us in the dark'*.

It was decided by the children to hide in the shadows of the bushes near the temple to watch the rituals. They stole away in the darkness silently.

The stage was set.

The villagers sat in a crescent circle near the neem tree in front of the *'Bhairav'* temple. There was a dreaded silence of trepidation and apprehension in the air. The restless crowd was abuzz in hushed whisper. The arrival of the 'Baba' was eagerly awaited.

There was a sudden huge silence when a shadowy dark tunic appeared with a staff in hand, and a red bundle slung over his shoulder, trailed by the superstitious minions from the village. He walked up to the neem tree and sat down, lowering his bundle on the ground. In silence he bent down to open the bundle, amidst chanting of *'magic spells and curses'*. Like some actor on a stage, the 'Tantric Baba' dramatically produced a *'human skull'* from his dark bundle. The villagers looked on spell bound. He laid down the white skull ceremoniously on a small red cloth he had spread on the ground. Incense stick was lit. The scent wafted across to the dazed audience.

No one noticed the four children creep up to witness the rituals.

They slid stealthily forward, inch by inch towards the ritual site. Holding their breath, the adventurous four ducked behind a bush.

'Shhhh..!' whispered Srilata, crouching among the shrubs. She stared intently at the ritual arrangements.

A girl lay bound within forty feet from the place where the children viewed the villagers. At first, there was a hum, and then it rose to a unison chanting of '*mantras*'.

The exorcist's rituals began!

There was a continuous clanging of a metal plate from somewhere in the distant forest. It was the Baba's assistant who soon appeared, holding a brass metal disc on one hand, and with the other, was hitting the circular metal disc in a rhythmic stroke with a wooden mallet, warning the dark spirits in the forest!

From where they were hidden, the four children, watched with uncertainty of the horror they were to witness.

The tantric Baba stood tall, dressed in his black robe with numerous beads dangling around his neck. He had a black bandana scarf tied on his head. The aura of venerated fear was felt in the dark rituals.

A fire was lit, and the Baba threw white '*luban*' serrata powder, crackling a curse. The flame leapt up instantly to lighten the faces of the silent audience, followed by the bellowing white smoke. He began his incantations - dreadful words to evoke fear in the ignorant rustics. The frightened villagers, with their palms pressed together, stood mesmerized like some frozen zombies, their lips quivering in some fearful hypnotic trance.

Amidst the incantations came the sudden eerie shrill scream of a girl in the dark night. A cold shiver ran down the spine of the assembled crowd.

The girl, who was bound, suddenly stirred. She was lifted up by some womenfolk to face the Baba. She was a frail girl of thirteen, emaciated either by starvation or illness, her eyes sunken in a delirious dream.

But suddenly, with a surge of amazing strength, the girl set herself free. She gave a yell of horrified nerve shattering scream. It paralyzed the minds of the onlookers.

'Eeeeeeeee....!'

Two women folk, struggled to hold and pin down the girl possessed with the evil spirit. She kicked and scratched in her hostility. The more she struggled to get free, the more violently did the tantric Baba sway from side to side.

In the red glow of the flames in front of the heat, the Baba's face was perspiring. He desperately clutched his heart, and finally with a faint groan of pain collapsed limp. He lay sprawled on the ground!

The clanging of the metal plate stopped. There was sudden silence, except for the fire that was crackling with the logs aflame. The villagers were clueless to what was happening. The girl was still screaming hysterically!

Was the evil spirit in her more powerful than the magic of the Tantric baba? The dark night was a muddled pandemonium.

The falcate audience stood up in stunned gasp! Some of the villagers stepped back in horror, slowly retreating towards the bushes in the rear. The Baba's assistant looked down helplessly at the fallen tantric 'Baba'.

The children too were taken aback in their appalled fear. They dived for cover in the underbrush. At the same instant, Srilata sprung out from the shadows of the bush. She lunged forward, bounding in big leaps from her hiding towards the tantric Baba. Everyone was astounded at the unexpected arrival of the girl. The children too were shocked! *Why was Srilata running towards the fallen tantric Baba?*

No one had the courage to move forward. They stood aghast in stunned silence. Their minds frozen both in horror and shock. They could not stop her, and allowed her to pass by, before they could recover from their dazed nerve.

Srilalata meanwhile, had reached the tantric Baba. He lay motionless, sprawled on the ground. His face pale white like a dead man. Srilata fell on her knees, and pressed both her hands vigorously on the Baba's chest, to revive him. She knew that the Baba had a cardiac arrest!

She recalled how her own father had died. Srilata pumped desperately! Finally as if by miracle, the tantric Baba's chest began to heave. He was alive! He opened his eyes, and looked up in bewilderment in a dazed state at Srilata. She helped the Baba to get up. He was soon rushed to the city hospital.

Later, the superstitious ignorant villagers learnt from the tantric Baba, how the girl had saved his life. He was indebted to her.

With a *'magic girl'* in the village, who would need a tantric Baba?

The villagers also learnt that the hysterical girl was not possessed by any evil spirit, but was suffering from schizophrenia- a mental ailment, due to severe psychiatric ailment of emotional instability and alienation. The ailing girl was sent to the Madavpur hospital for the psychiatric disorder. She recovered, and returned to the village in a few months.

The insane village of Shivpur became sane forever!

*

If superstition enters, the brain is gone.

They alone live who live for others, the rest are more dead than alive.

- **Swami Vivekananda**

BELEH

If money help a man to do good to others, it is of some value; but if not, it is simply a mass of evil, and the sooner it is got rid of, the better.

- **Swami Vivekananda**

BELEH

Beleh, the master story teller sat on the top landing of the curved stairway, his hands cupped on to his cheeks, viewing the hall below. He was awake, consciously believing that at that moment, he had fallen asleep, yet was aware that he was dreaming, and felt like a fictional character, in the flesh of 'majesty', to be installed soon.

He mused about his pranks, yet could not reason out, why he was reprimanded by the elders. They tolerated his pranks with a smile; yet frowned.

The loud ticking of the grandfather clock in the hall below, abruptly whirled with the cog wheels turning to strike, a melodious somber clear deep resonance of five repeated sonorous strokes. Beleh counted each gong. It was five - the time for children to be out from home, after the hot noon, to 'Beleh's durbar' to assemble; the interlude, before the evening pranks were to be performed, by every child in the neighborhood.

Beleh seemed to have opened his eyes of celebration on a Saturday, but was concentrated to make it Sunday. A day to celebrate the joy of childhood. Before him on the landing below, was the vacant hall for his subjects. It was a child's world in which he lived, yet played his role as the king. He loved the stage, nor lacked the slightest talent as majesty, and used to get a flawless performance from the young brats from neighborhood, as 'subjects'.

He knew he was awake. His soft big eyes were compassionate, yet there was a glint of innocence and mischief that parents see, and often condone as harmless, the naughty pranks of their loving children. The Dutta family overlooked Beleh's innocent mischief. It was a childhood, both amusing and restrained, available only to minds, unspoilt by adult experience.

Dutta mansion was in a posh locality of respectable 'Bhadrolok', at Shimla Pally – the residence locality of the city social elites, where every passerby treaded softly like tiny impersonal being. The street vendors, who shouted to sell their wares at other localities, became indecipherable toned down calls, as they crossed the mansion hall. The neighborhood children lived far away from the solemn street.

The previous night's party, organized by his father, was over. The barrister guests from the court had celebrated his father's success: a five year protracted civil case of a Zamindar. The judge had rejected a poor peasant's petition. If the peasant and his family had gone hungry at night; the guests had dined. Beleh, after overhearing the repeated arguments of their artistic success and failures, had settled down in his cozy bed, closed his eyes, with sleep overtaking his consciousness. Beleh at that tender age, knew not the peasant, yet was sympathetic for the poor human soul.

Gradually, the sound of the merry makers was wrapped gently away from his ears, effacing his memories, fading each of the faces, forgetting even his own name, back in the beginning, in the vision of the mythological god, meditating atop the white expanse on the Himalayas. He felt that he could choose to be anyone. .. any character… a naughty child, a wandering monk, a farmer, a majestic king…or even Shiva, the Lord!

The guests had left, some inebriated, ushered away by their attendants.

The vast hall was now empty.

The massive front door lay open, folded inward. An engraved brass name plate on the door read: *Barrister* Vishwanath *Dutta, Calcutta High Court. Shimla Pally* - the abode of a generous father, who was tolerant of the young lad's pranks, yet with a progressive outlook in social and religious matters, frowned at orthodoxy. He commanded respect in the social circle.

The crepuscular light flooded the hall, to a rich glistening sheen on the chequered black and white marble floor, in the twilight. The floor had been scrubbed clean by the domestic servants.

The winding stairway was built with seasoned mahogany wood, a magnificent structure that lured the neighborhood young boys to the 'durbar' of Beleh.

A faint thin shadow slowly stretched on the floor.

The first to meekly enter was Dolu, with a slight limp and front tooth missing. He was soon followed by a chattering group of the neighborhood gang - Robin, the head master's son; Kanchan, the nitwit son of the city postmaster; Anand, the police superintendent's son, Arun, and finally Bolu, the fat stubborn child of the local physician. They were all from respectable families, but

lacked the mannerism in their rambunctious endeavors. The chatter reduced to a soft mellow greeting as they stood in front of Beleh – the majesty!

'Your majesty, we salute you!' said Bolu, bowing courteously. Taking count from him, the other subjects paid their respect. They stood like courtiers in two rows, looking up at Beleh.

'I thank you for the greetings. The king's court may begin', declared Beleh with a clap that resounded in the huge hall. Each subject took a step forward to state his name and declare – *'Present your Highness!'*

When the attendance was taken, Beleh enquired from Anand.

'What is the first charge Wazir?'

Anand, who was designated the Wazir in the past meeting, stood dumbfounded.

What charge was Beleh talking about?

He fumbled a few words.

'I..I…don't known….'

In that hilarious moment, Robin was outspoken. *'The password!'*

Every one present had to walk up to the Wazir and whisper the password –*'Zomlu'*

When it was Dolu's turn, the poor boy stood silent. He did not know the password as he was absent for a month.

'A spy..a spy!' shouted Anand clutching Dolu's wrist.

'Beleh, we have to punish Dolu for his absence!'

Dolu was absent for a month from Beleh's Durbar. He was ordered to explain. Poor Dolu trembled to relate his bad time. He stood agape, his mouth open to expose his missing front tooth, He did not know how to begin.

'Now tell us what happened?' enquired Beleh, with a compassionate tone of assurance that he would not punish Dolu.

'Your majesty,' replied Dolu, bowing down courteously. He turned to a side to face the six anxious subjects and narrated his *'unforeseen'* accident

'I was in a hurry to join the gang of Shimla pally....'

The gang listened in rapt attention.

Dolu's story:

'It was after my breakfast that fateful morning, when I had rushed out to join the gang for the 'royal football match', with the players from the kingdom of Manektala, the neighborhood street gang, that tragedy struck. I was hoping to go to join the play as a goal keeper. I had grabbed my bike and rushed, but as I crossed the street, a carriage came down the street. I panicked, hit the front brake and fell forward, taking one somersault, and fell sprawled on the street. I had lost consciousness.

When I awoke, I was in the hospital. I did not remember anything, well yes. ... I had to play a game, but it would not be possible, because I had broken a leg and a tooth!

I spent a few days in the hospital, and then at home in bed for a month. During that time, my only thought was of my friends and the 'king's durbar'. A few of my friends had visited me daily. Chatting with them; gave me every information I had missed- I was not told of the new pass word.'

Beleh sat listening with his eyes closed picturing the

events and scenes as Dolu related every detail. He sometimes smiled : sometimes scowled. He finally opened his eyes, shifted to a side and sat erect. He sat like a 'majesty' listening to the stories of his subjects. It was the most charming childrens' world, overwhelming moment, every second, to continue indefinitely.

Arun, who stood near Bolu nudged the fat boy gently with his elbow, to stop him digging his nose. Bolu almost fell over. Beleh and other children let out a hearty laugh. They radiated a sincere, primary, overflowing joy. Beleh's voice did not falter or fade. It was soothing, soft and assuring.

'Well you are pardoned. Remember the new password - Zomlu,' said Beleh raising his hand as a gesture of blessing to both Dolu and Bolu!

Their stories, although intruding on a fictional world, stuck to the utopian, certain to keep breathing in reality. It was to avoid distractions. It was now time for the children to climb up the stairs to huddle and sit near the king. They clamoured up the stairs for the story session.

Beleh's mother came in view. She paused to see the assembled children. She smiled as assurance, to the concentration that appeared on her brows, that the naughty children would be away from mischief, with Beleh narrating a story. Some of Beleh's tales were her own, that her son now proudly narrated to the gang.

Beleh noticed his mother standing. He remained silent. It was only when the gracious lady had moved away silently towards the inner part of the hall, that the master story teller cleared his throat, and began to tell his story.

The children listened in rapt attention, entranced by the master story teller.

Beleh took them to a wonderland – to the immense world, extending beyond the hall where they sat.

Beleh continued - *'I'll tell you a story about a lazy man...'*

Beleh's story:

'There was a poor man who was very lazy and yet wanted money. In his childhood he had heard of ghosts and genies. He thought if he could get hold of one of them, he might command the genie to bring him anything he desired. The man was very impatient, and set about searching for some magician, to get hold of one genie. He went about searching for someone who could tell him how to get to a genie. He asked everyone he met, if they knew of any magician with great powers.

One day, while wandering out in the outskirts of the city, he met a group of hunters going for a hunt in the forest. He enquired from them. 'Brothers, you go into the forest everyday. Have you ever seen any genie there?'

'No', the hunters replied. 'However, there is a hermit in the forest who has powers to catch any ghost or a genie'

The lazy man was overjoyed with the information. He did not stop for a moment to thank them. After they had shown him the path to follow, he hurried forward to reach the hermit's hermitage in the forest. He truddged the entire day. It was nearly sunset, when he reached the hermit's hut.

He saw an old hermit with a white overflowing beard, sitting on a mat under a tree near the hut. The hermit was in deep meditation.

The lazy man sat and waited patiently for some time, and then became restless. He began to cough to distract the hermit. The hermit opened his eyes and saw the man standing in front of him.

'What do you want?' The hermit enquired, 'and who are you?'

At this, the man began to weep and implore.

'I'm a poor man who has no work. I implore you to catch a genie so that my needs are fulfilled.'

The hermit's visage turned to a sullen scowl. 'Go away, and don't trouble me.'

The man was however very adamant. He waited the

entire night and the next morning. The kind hermit at last gave way to his pleadings and tenacity.

'Take this Talisman and wear it round your neck', said the hermit. The hermit took out a charm with a black string and handed it over to the man. 'However, you must repeat the magic word –'Atantu' thrice, and a genie will appear at your command. But beware, if you fail to give him any task, he'll be your master and may imprison you forever!'

The man was delighted. In his excitement he did not heed to the warning.

'I'll give him endless long task to fulfill all my desires. I have nothing to fear', said the excited man. He then hurriedly left for his own home. He reached home, and sat down to pull out the charm, and carefully wore it around his neck. He next repeated the magic word 'Atantu' thrice.

Lo! A huge genie appeared before him. The man was taken aback, but remembered that the genie was his servant. He could command anything like a master.

The genie bowed down and boomed out loudly – 'What does master desire from me?'

The man was amazed, and for a moment began trembling at the sight of the genie. His words were choked. He finally blurted out the first thought that came to him – 'Build a big house for me!'

In an instant his home had turned into a palace. The man was overjoyed, and then in his excitement commanded numerous tasks one after another.

'Furniture, horse carriage, garden, swimming pool, servants, shoes, clothes....!'

Words of command came tumbling out from his mouth. They were instantly supplied by the genie.

The man became more and more greedy.

'Bring me gold, money, wealth', the man cried out in excitement.

The genie obeyed instantly.

Finally, the man was exhausted, and had nothing to order for. The genie sat in front of him smiling mischievously, waiting to imprison the man with a rope that appeared in his hands. The man began to tremble. He remembered the hermit's warning-'If you do not give task to him, the genie will imprison you forever!'

The man began to panic. He was now truly frightened.

The genie gleefully looked at the man with mischief twinkling in his eyes. The genie rubbed his hands in delight!

'Master give me a task, else I'll imprison you!'

The poor man thought frantically, but alas had nothing to order in his muddled thoughts. He was truly frightened, and started to run away. He kept running as fast as he could towards the forest with the genie harrying behind –'Give me some task. Give me some task. Give me some task!'

The man was exhausted when he reached the forest where the hermit lived. He fell at the hermit's feet and pleaded mercifully - 'Oh wise hermit save me. The genie will imprison me as I have no task for him.'

The man began to cringe in fear.

The hermit smiled, 'You fool. I warned you. Now

see where your greed and laziness has led you to. There is no moment to loose. Command the genie to take back everything one by one.'

The man obeyed, and gave the genie the task to take away everything that he had desired. When the entire task was completed, the hermit told the man to order the genie to straighten the tail of a dog that lived with the hermit.

The man commanded, and the genie obeyed. However to the genie's amazement, whenever he tried to straighten the tail, it curled up again. The task was a perpetual one. The wise hermit had tricked the genie to a lifelong task!

The man thanked the hermit and returned the magic talisman.

'I don't want anything that can cause trouble. I am happy to be poor.'

He paid his respect to the hermit and returned home. He had learnt his lesson. He now found work and was not lazy anymore.'

Having related the story, the bewildered children returned to reality from the magic world. At that instance the Grandfather clock struck the melodious metallic resounding time. It was six in the evening- the time to return home; while for some, to continue their pranks outside, in the lap of nature.

Beleh dismissed the gang.

It was now Beleh's time to search for *Hanuman*! He went out with Dolu to the nearby garden. It was the time for his exuberant energy to be free - to face the challenges he loved. He was told of the spirits that roamed freely in the dusk, but did not believe in such superstition. He never had seen one!

He was drawn to the garden, and stayed late evening, because a priest had told him where to find god *Hanuman*. Beleh therefore, every evening, always went to a grove where a champak tree branch offered the young lad, a place to swing freely like a monkey. He was a little monkey himself, wanting to join the *'Vanar sena'* of god *Hanuman*. He loved to pluck the champak flowers, and break branches like the monkeys. Beleh loved to hang down with his legs, swinging like a nocturnal bat!

The irritated owner of the grove, exasperated by the young lad's pranks, tried to frighten him-

'Beleh, if you hang like that on the champak tree, a ghost that lives in the grove will break your neck.' Not intimidated easily, Beleh merely smiled and continued to swing. Dolu however was freighted. He spoke nervously to his friend. *'Everyone in our street tells the same story.'*

Beleh kept swinging and finally dropped down to face Dolu – *'Silly! What goofs you all are? If the ghost existed, it would have broken my neck much earlier. See it's still intact!'*

The two children soon left the garden. The sun had disappeared over the horizon. The evening sun was sinking, filtering radiance through the thickets. The sky lit up to a golden tinge, and then gradually dimmed to a purple red glow. The fading light of the dusk brought birds to roost in the thick woods. The evening star blazed in the descending evening dark sky.

Nobody who was in the place would be mistaken of the mischievous smile of victory, as the young lad skipped merrily along towards Dutta mansion.

*

The world is the great gymnasium where we come to make ourselves strong.

- **Swami Vivekananda**

GLOSSARY

Parables : a story to relate some truth
Saraswati river: a river that once flowed in north India
Meandering : movement in a winding course
Glistening : shining
Biodiversity : plants and wildlife in the world
Flora : vegetation/flowers
Fauna: animals in the world
Abundance : plenty
Bounties : reward/ sum paid for capturing
Pilgrims: journey undertaken to religious place
Tranquility : peace/calm
Quench : satisfy by drinking
Symphony : musical composition of a full ochestra
Evoke : to recall in mind
Fragrance: sweet smell
Rishi : a sage
Ashrams : hermitage
Gurukuls : hermitage/ a place of learning by disciples under a sage
Revered : respected
Marshal arts : traditional combat sports
Conjure : cause something to appear by magic
Ascetics : a recluse who abstains from indulgence
Hermitage : a hermit's dwelling
Celibacy : abstaining physical relationship/ marriage
Austerity : sternness of manners

Vedic : relating to Vedas
Tedious : tiresome
Scriptures : sacred writings
Imparting : teach/make known
Disciple : student
Wards : child under a guardian
Guruma : wife of a sage/Rishi
Precocious : certain abilities developed in a child
Serene: peaceful
Frolicking : to play lively
Environ : surround
Vibrant : full of energy
Pomp : splendid display
Incessant : continuous without stopping
Flippant : thoughtless
Sober : not drunk
Somber: stern/serious
Tranquil : peace
Nocturnal : nightly
Apparitions : ghost like
Quipped : make a witty remark
Valour : courage
Begets : to bring out/results in
Solemn : serious
Huddled: to sit close together
Outwitted : out smarted
Intently: keenly
Mantras : magic spells
Threshold :the doorway entrance
Ablutions : washing/purification by cleaning
Inquisitive : curiosity
Dispel : remove /drive away
Inched : to move very slowly/creep
Pondered : to think
Nagged : annoy
Impulse : sudden inclination

Stubbornly: obstinately
Ridiculous : foolish
Giggling : short spasmodic laugh
Boisterous : energetic
Commotion : uproar
Antics : tricks
Ignominy : shame
awry : muddled
Beckoned : called
Dawned: made aware
Agape: wonderstruck with mouth open
Ignorance : lack of knowledge
Dedication : devotion
Delusion: illusion
Effulgent : radiant light
Naren : Narendra
Musty : moldy
Desolation : loneliness
Soggy : damp
Faucet : tap
Salvage : recover
Props : support
Eerie : scary
Foliage : undergrowth
Hue : color
Ravens : crow
Undertakers: a funeral director
Succor : relief
Wetland : marshland
Profuse : plentiful
Bagnan : a village in Bengal
Nawab : a feudal lord
Dilapidated : old/broken
Impoverished : poor
Despondence : sadness
Derisory : pitiful

Fury : rage
Damodar : a large river in south Bengal
Holy ritual: religious ceremony
River of sorrow: Damodar river in south Bengal
Upanayana ceremony : the ceremony of coming to age
Abandoned : discarded/neglected
Winsome : charming
Untouchable : impervious
Outskirts : outer edge
Menial: unskilled
Murky : muddy
Zamindars : feudal landlords
Initiated : to begin
Brahamalogy: the study of Brahama (god of creation)
Sanctified : made holy/sacred
Zealot : believer
Orthodoxy : convention
Penury : poverty
Three strands in the sacred thread: a religious thread worn after holy initiation.
Abode: house
Meager : too little
Sari : a long length of cloth worn by Indian women
Satiate: satisfy
Persistent: constant
Pang: heart ache/emotionally hurt
Tortuously: painfully
Impulsive : instinctive/ wreckless/to act without thinking
Ethereal: ghostly
Bleak : without hope
Goddess of prosperity : Goddess Laxmi
Kuleen Brahamin : A Brahamin of pure lineage
Propitious : favourable
Auspicious : fortunate
Temerity: boldness
Ardent: passionate

Venerated : respected
Goddess Kali: a goddess
Shiva: god
Vengeance: revenge
Cremated: to reduce dead to ashes by fire
Chanting: utter religious recitations
Clamored: to rush towards
Morsel: crumb
Frail: weak
Gullible: innocent
Rustic : villager
Serpentine queue: a long queue
Prasad: eatable offerings to gods
Linen: cotton
Siesta: afternoon nap
Obese : fat
Akimbo: arms folded
Kurta/dhoti : Indian shirt/ length of cloth worn around lower body
Aura : sensation/atmosphere
Domineering : bossy
Menacing : threatening
Demeanor : conduct
Writ: written
Lineage : direct descendent in heredity
Social sanction: restricted in society
Absolve : resolve
Social stigma : social discrimination by birth or profession
Matrimonial alliance: marriage proposal
Savior : liberator
Condemned : fated
Ostracized : detested
Humble : modest
Dwelling: habitat
Dowry: money/ trousseau brought by the bride after marriage
Redeem : rescue

Nuptial ties: marriage
Consummated : fruition
Redemption : salvation
Prostrate: to lay flat
Obeisance : bend in reverence
Perpetual : everlasting
Importunate : persistent
Solemnized: to perform a holy bond
Affirmation: assertion
Sandhyavandanum: evening invocation
Non chalant: dispassionate
Compassion : kindness
Servile : submissive to master
Chauvinist : dogmatist
Elated: jubilant
Rekindled: to excite
Serenading : singing
Ritual : ceremony
Transition: shift
Endowed : gifted
Veda : ancient system/scriptures
Pious : holy
Krishna: a god
Guru Dakshina: fees paid by disciple
Peepal: a large tree
Maya: illusion
Ordained : intended/ designed
Retaliation: reprisal
Inundated: flooded
Anaconda: a huge snake
Rampage: run amok
Ignorant : uninformed
Appeased : pacify
Sparse : meager
Kalbaishaki : tropical rain
Pestilence : disease

Vodooism : practice of black magic
Wizen : wizard
Tantric Baba : exorcist who uses tantra magic
Emaciated: thin
Jejune : immature
Dusk: evening
Sanforized : shrunken
Gaunt : skinny
Pithu: a game by piling/wrecking seven stones
Feticide: killing the fetus
Druid : a class of people who use herbs for cure
Hatt : a village market
Heart seizure: heart attack
Usurped : to seize office/power illegally
Bhairav : a demon god
Scraggy : scrawny/lean
Greesham: summer
Ominious: portentous
Lingered: stay back/ tarry
Pall : dark covering
Conch : a large spiral sea shell
Pariah: outsider
Lurking : unobserved/to move furtively
Neem : a type of herbal tree
Incantations : ritual chanting
Hysterical: panic striken
Tortuous convulsions : painful twisting
Swoon: faint
Exorcist : a healer who can drive out spirits from patients
Bandana: scarf
Luban : herbal frankinscence
Zombies: reanimated dead people
Hypnotic trance : psychological state
Delirious : confused/feverish
Falcate : curved/semicircular
Cardiac arrest : heart attack

Schizopherenia : mental disorder
Psychiatric : mental health
Alienation : isolation
Insane : mad
Reprimand : warning/scolding
Abruptly: suddenly
Resonance : reverberation
Durbar: royal court
Restrained : controlled
Bhadralok : gentlemen
Indecipherable : unreadable
Shimla Pally: locality in north Kolkata
Protracted: prolonged
Petition : appeal
Mythological : fairy tale/ legendary fabulous story
Inebriated : drunk
Crepuscular: evening light
Twilight : evening light
Mahogany : rich reddish-brown wood
Rambunctious : boisterous/lively
Endeavour: attempt/effort
Wazir: Prime Minister in Mogul royal court
Manektala : a locality in north Kolkata city
Utopian : idealized perfection
Concentration : attentiveness
Genie : apparition that can perform tasks
Tenacity : doggedness
Atantu: invented word
Hanuman : a monkey god
Champak: a tree
Dutta mansion: house where young Vivekananda lived